CONTENTS

Play football!   4

Get started   6

The referee and rules   8

Control it!   10

Pass it!   12

Passing and moving   14

Head it!   16

Shoot!   18

Play in goal   20

Good defence   22

Develop your skills   24

Fouls and free kicks   26

Making the team   28

Glossary   30

Resources   31

Index   32

PLAY FOOTBALL!

Football (also called soccer) is the world's most popular team sport. A full game is played for two halves, each lasting 45 minutes, with a 15-minute half-time break. Two teams, each with 11 players, compete for the ball, aiming to score goals.

PLAYING THE GAME

Football is a fast-moving game involving lots of running. The team with the ball attacks the other team's goal, trying to score.

1 Footballers run using small taps of their feet to keep the ball under control. Players can also use their chest and head to control the ball.

2 Passing the ball moves it around the pitch. The team with the ball attacks ands tries to get close to the other team's goal.

3 A good pass puts this attacker clear of the other team's players. He takes a strong shot at goal.

GET SPORTY

Football

Edward Way

WAYLAND

Published in 2013 by Wayland

Copyright © Wayland 2013

Wayland
338 Euston Road
London NW1 3BH

Wayland Australia
Level 17/207 Kent Street
Sydney NSW 2000

Editor: Nicola Edwards
Designer: www.rawshock.co.uk

The author and publisher would
like to thank Broadstone Hall
Primary School and Joe, Steven,
Reece, Jack, Aaron, Shanice,
Elliot, James, Tom, Eloise and
Rhiann for their help with the
photographs for this book.

British Library Cataloguing in
Publication Data
Way, Edward.
   Football. -- (Get sporty)
   1. Soccer--Juvenile literature.
   I. Title II. Series
   796.3'34-dc22
ISBN: 978 0 7502 7167 7

Picture acknowledgements
All photographs by Clive Gifford
apart from p9 Michael Wicks, p15
p17 Nicolas Asfouri/AFP/Getty
Images; p19 Liu Jin/AFP/Getty
Images; p25 Denis Doyle/Getty
Images; p27 Juan Barreto/AFP/
Getty Images; p29 Adrian Dennis/
AFP/Getty Images.

Printed in China.

Wayland is a division of Hachette
Children's Books, an Hachette UK
company.
www.hachette.co.uk

4 The goalkeeper is the only player on a team who is allowed to handle the ball. Here, a goalkeeper makes a diving save.

GOAL!

To score a goal, the ball has to completely cross the goal line between the two goal posts.

If a goal is scored, the game is restarted with a kick-off from the centre of the pitch.

ATTACKERS AND DEFENDERS

A team lines up with rows of defenders, midfielders and forwards. When a team doesn't have the ball, it defends. Its players try to stop goals being scored and win the ball back fairly. All the players in a football team must work together.

A defender (right) and the goalkeeper work together to try to clear the ball away from their goal.

GET STARTED

Football is played on a rectangular pitch. Most pitches are made of grass but some artificial pitches are used, especially indoors.

THE PITCH

Pitches vary in size depending on whether they are used for a full or smaller-sided game. All pitches have similar markings including a penalty area. A goalkeeper can only handle the ball inside his or her own penalty area.

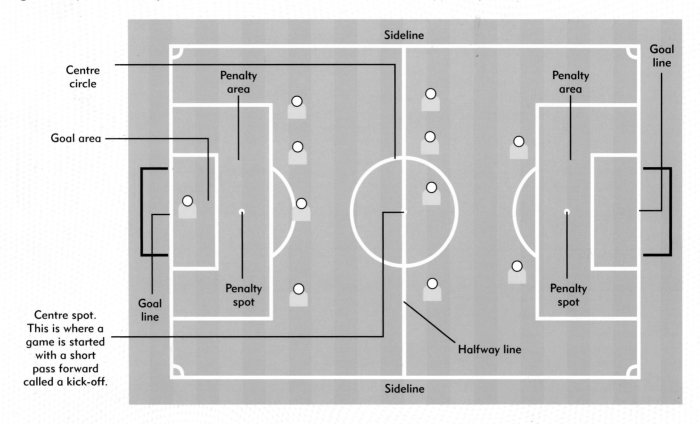

Centre circle

Penalty area

Sideline

Goal line

Penalty area

Goal area

Centre spot. This is where a game is started with a short pass forward called a kick-off.

Goal line

Penalty spot

Halfway line

Penalty spot

Sideline

THE GOAL

A goal is made up of two vertical posts, a crossbar running along the top and a net. This player is making sure the net is fixed securely before a match.

FOOTBALL KIT

The clothing a footballer wears when playing a match is called the team kit or strip. All the players in a team, except the goalkeeper, wear a matching strip. Footballers often wear a tracksuit over their kit to keep warm and dry before and after a match or training.

Tie the laces of your football boots really securely. Boots have studs on the sole for playing on grass or small pimples for playing on artificial surfaces.

Players wear shorts, long socks and a football shirt which can be long or short sleeved.

Goalkeepers wear a different coloured shirt from their team-mates and goalkeeping gloves which help them to grip the ball.

This player is putting on a shinpad underneath his football socks. Shinpads protect the front, bony part, of your lower leg from kicks and knocks.

THE REFEREE AND RULES

A referee and two assistants are in charge of running a football match. They make sure that the players follow the rules of the game.

IN AND OUT OF PLAY

When the ball goes out of play, the team that didn't touch it last receives the ball. If the ball crosses goal line, the referee will award either a corner or a goal kick. If it crosses a sideline, the game is restarted with a throw-in.

TAKING A THROW-IN

1 The player takes the ball back over his head with both hands and makes sure his feet are on or behind the sideline.

2 His hands are spread around the sides of the ball as he brings it forward over his head. He aims to throw the ball to a team-mate who will bring it under control.

3 After releasing the ball, the player can run back on to the pitch. Another player from either team must touch the ball before the thrower can touch it again.

THE BACKPASS RULE

You can pass the ball back to your goalkeeper but remember:

A goalkeeper cannot pick up the ball if a team-mate kicks it back to him.

The goalkeeper must kick the ball.

TOP TIP Unless you are a goalkeeper you are not allowed to use your hands or your arms to control the ball. If you do, the referee will signal a handball and award a free kick (see page 27) to the other team.

YELLOW CARD

A yellow card is a warning given by the referee for a serious break of the rules. A player who receives two yellow cards in a game is sent off. The game continues with his or her team one player short.

CONTROL IT!

A football can bounce all over a pitch. To be able to pass it, shoot or run with it well, a footballer needs to bring the ball under control quickly.

UNDER CONTROL

To control the ball you often have to slow it down as it arrives. You can do this by keeping relaxed the part of your body the ball strikes, and moving that part back or down as the ball comes to you. Here are three different ways of controlling the ball: with the side of your foot, your chest and your thigh.

1 The inside of your foot can control a bouncing ball. Lift your foot off the ground. Turn your foot so the inside of your boot meets the ball.

2 As the ball arrives, take your foot back to soften the contact. The ball should drop at your feet ready for your next move.

 TOP TIP
You can stop a rolling ball by placing your foot on top of it. This is called trapping. Be careful not to stamp down on the ball or it may slip away.

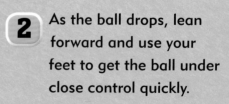

CHEST CONTROL

1 You can use your chest to control a high ball. Lean back as the ball arrives. Make sure the ball does not hit your arms.

2 As the ball drops, lean forward and use your feet to get the ball under close control quickly.

THIGH CONTROL

1 As the ball falls towards you, raise your leg at the knee and lift it high. Your thigh should be almost level with the ground when the ball arrives.

2 Pull your leg back and down as the ball connects to soften its landing. Watch the ball as it drops to your feet.

During a game, try to stay aware of the play going on around you as the ball arrives. Be ready to run, shoot or pass as soon as you have the ball under control.

TOP TIP

Play passing and controlling games with friends, such as keepy-uppy where players use their feet, legs, chest and head to keep the ball off of the ground. You can also practise on your own by kicking a football against a wall at different heights and using different parts of your body to control it as it rebounds.

PASS IT!

Passing is the quickest way to move the football around the pitch. It is the most common move in football. At the final of Euro 2008 between Germany and Spain, there were 859 passes in a single game!

RIGHT EACH TIME

You need to be able to pass well with both your feet. Aim to hit each pass with the right amount of force so that the ball reaches the player receiving it and is easy to control. The most frequently used type of pass, particularly over shorter distances, is the sidefoot pass.

1 The player runs up to the ball. He makes sure he is balanced and keeps his eyes on the ball.

2 He positions his non-kicking foot beside the ball and the weight of his body over the ball as he swings his leg back.

3 He swings his leg forwards to push the side of his foot through the football. The ball should zip across the top of the pitch.

4 The player watches the ball as his kicking leg follows through in the direction of the pass.

Try to strike through the middle of the ball with the whole of the side of your foot. Hitting the bottom of the ball will send the ball high into the air.

THE INSTEP PASS

You can make longer passes using your instep - the part of your boot where the laces are.

Put your standing foot beside the ball and point your kicking foot down at the ankle as it swings back and forward.

TOP TIPS To send the ball to a team-mate who is nearby, you can use the outside part of your boot to make a very short flick pass. You flick your foot at the ankle and push the ball away a short distance to the side.

Most footballers have a foot they prefer to use to pass and kick the ball. It's important to practise hard with your weaker foot so that you are comfortable passing with both.

PASSING AND MOVING

For a pass to be successful, team-mates must get into space on the pitch where they can receive the ball. Quick, accurate passing between players can get the ball past opponents and close to goal for a chance to score.

GETTING FREE

Players need to know how to escape from opponents who are marking or guarding them. You can use changes of running speed and direction to get free of an opponent.

1 The attacker (in the striped shirt) has moved to her left and the defender moves to cover her.

2 She changes direction, pushing hard off her left foot to move to the right.

3 The defender has to stop and follow her but will take time to recover.

4 Once the attacker changes direction, she sprints to get into space to receive the ball.

THE WALL PASS

The one-two or wall pass is a good way to get the ball past an opposing player.

1 One player passes the ball to a team-mate.

2 As soon as the ball leaves her foot, she sprints past the opposing player

3 A team-mate receives the ball and passes the ball behind the opponent for the first player to run onto.

PRO PLAY

David Beckham, shown here playing for Milan, crosses the ball during the 2009 Serie A match between AC Milan and US Citta di Palermo. When you are passing to players on the run, try to pass the ball ahead of them, so that they do not have to stop to collect the ball.

HEAD IT!

Heading the ball is an important skill both in attack and defence. A player can score a goal with a header, while defenders often have to head the ball away from danger.

MAKING A HEADER

Some young players are nervous of heading at first, but if it's done well it doesn't hurt. If you prefer, you can start practising with a soft foam ball and work up to heading a real football.

1 The player pulls his head and upper body back. His eyes watch the ball right onto his head.

2 He springs up into the air and pushes his head forwards to meet the ball with the middle of his forehead.

3 He keeps his neck muscles firm as he sends the ball away.

4 After making the header, the player lands safely on both feet. He bends his knees to cushion his landing and is ready to continue playing.

TOP TIP You can score goals with headers. Aim the ball downwards with your head positioned over the ball to keep it on target.

When the ball is ahead of you and cannot be reached with a regular header or kick, you can choose to launch yourself forward to make a diving header, as Chelsea's John Terry has done here.

DEFENSIVE HEADERS

Defenders sometimes need to head the ball away from danger.

1 This defender (left) has timed his jump to meet the ball ahead of an opponent. He is aiming to head the ball at the top of his jump.

2 His head connects with the lower half of the ball to send the ball upwards and forwards away from his goal.

SHOOT!

When you get the chance to shoot at goal, keep calm and focused. This will help you to choose exactly where to aim your shot. Try to send the ball away from the goalkeeper and into the corner of the goal.

TAKING A SHOT

You may be tempted to kick the ball as hard as you can, but you must keep your shot on target so control is important too.

1 This player is about to shoot. He has chosen where to aim and has his eyes on the ball.

2 As he swings his kicking foot back, his other foot is next to the ball. He does not lean back as this can make the ball fly too high.

3 He swings his leg through to strike the ball cleanly, keeping his eye on the ball.

4 The player stays aware of what happens to the ball as it leaves his foot. If it bounces off another player or off the goal posts or crossbar, he may get a second chance to attack.

Volleys (when you kick the ball in the air before it has bounced) are often used for powerful shots from long distances.

1 This player watches the ball as it travels towards him.

2 He lifts his kicking leg up and back with his foot pointed down.

3 He swings his foot through so that his laces connect with the ball while it is still in the air.

TOP TIPS

Sometimes, team-mates may be in a better position to score than you. Instead of shooting, you can pass to them to give your team a better chance of scoring.

Don't get upset if you take a shot and miss. Get back into the game – another chance is likely to come your way soon.

You can practise shooting in training or on your own. Place cones on the goal line and aim your shots at the corners of the goal between the cones and the goal post.

PRO PLAY

German football star Birgit Prinz shoots and scores against Brazil at the 2008 Olympics. Prinz has scored over 125 goals for Germany.

PLAY IN GOAL

Goalkeepers have the crucial job of stopping goals being scored. They stay alert throughout a game, instructing their defenders, saving shots and passing the ball to team-mates.

SAVING THE BALL

Try to get in line with the direction of the ball. Positioning your body behind the ball will give you a second barrier to stop the ball should you fumble it with your hands. Gather the ball into your body to protect it.

1 This keeper is in the ready position in the middle of his goal. He watches to see where the ball is and is ready to move in any direction. He starts to move to his right.

2 This goalkeeper dives to his right to stop a shot. He pushes off his foot closest to the direction in which he wants to dive.

3 After stretching out his arms to get his hands around the ball, he gathers the ball in towards his chest.

Here, the goalkeeper makes a high save. He watches the ball with his arms stretched upwards, and spreads his fingers wide around the back and sides of the ball.

ORGANISATION

As a goalkeeper, you have a great view of how the game is going. You should organise your team-mates when defending by shouting clear orders to them.

TOP TIP

If the ball is too high or too wide for you to gather in with both hands, try to punch it away, striking firmly through the middle of the ball.

DISTRIBUTION

Once goalkeepers have the ball in their hands, they have six seconds to release it with a kick or a throw. This is called distribution.

Goalkeepers can make longer throws by bowling the ball out overarm.

This goalkeeper uses an underarm throw to roll the ball across the surface of the pitch.

Goalkeepers sometimes kick the ball out of their hands a long way up the pitch.

GOOD DEFENCE

When your team loses the ball, it has to defend. The aim of defence is to stop a goal being scored against you and to win the ball back fairly.

TACKLING

Tackling is removing the ball from the control of an opposing player by using your foot. Your foot must strike the ball not the opponent or it will be a foul.

1 A defender (in red) moves in to challenge an opponent with the ball.

2 As he arrives, he turns his foot so that the inside of it will connect with the ball.

3 Positioning his bodyweight over the ball, he strikes firmly through the centre of the ball.

4 The defender has to react quickly when the ball comes free so that he can reach the ball first and get it under control.

MARKING

One important part of defence is marking. Players stand close to an opponent and move with them, trying to deny them the space to receive the ball.

When you are marking an opponent, keep an eye both on where the ball is and on the player you are marking. Be ready to move sharply in any direction.

TOP TIP

If the ball gets wedged between the feet, you can lower your foot and lift and roll the ball up and over the opponent's boot.

WORKING TOGETHER

Every player in a team should defend. This includes the attackers who chase down opponents with the ball and try to force them into making a mistake. Team-mates must work together in defence to stop an attack.

1 A defender closes down an opponent with the ball. He has run in to guard and delay him.

2 A team-mate runs in to support the first defender, in case the attacker gets past him.

3 With support behind, the defender can now try to win the ball with a tackle.

DEVELOP YOUR SKILLS

Footballers need a large range of skills to perform well. These include learning how to shield the ball and how to move with the ball under control.

SHIELDING

Often when the ball comes to you, an opponent will be following close behind. When this happens you can turn your body to shield the ball from your opponent.

1 This player receives the ball, gets it under control…

2 …and moves his body so that it is between his opponent and the football.

3 The player keeps his body between the opponent and the ball as he moves to stop the opponent reaching the ball with his foot. He must not push or foul him.

4 He controls the ball with small taps of his feet as he turns. He looks to make a pass but there isn't an obvious one.

5 So, instead, he sprints away with the ball ahead of him. When you run with the ball, keep your head up watching the positions of players ahead of you. If there is lots of space ahead of you, push the ball further ahead so that you can run onto it.

PRO PLAY

When the ball goes out over the goal line and the defending team touched it last, the attacking team is awarded a corner. This is a free kick from the corner quadrant, as shown here being taken by Shunsuke Nakamura. Corner-takers practise hard so that they send the ball accurately towards their team-mates.

TOP TIP

Practise dribbling with the ball by moving it using taps and nudges. Players swerve and move from side to side to try to beat a defender as they dribble.

FOULS AND FREE KICKS

Everyone expects some contact between players during a game. But some actions are fouls. These include kicking, barging or tripping another player.

FOUL!

When referees see a foul, they blow their whistle to stop the game. The team who was fouled usually receives a free kick. If a serious foul occurs and the player who was fouled is in his or her opponent's penalty area, the referee usually awards a penalty instead. Here are some examples of fouls.

PUSHING

1 As a high ball comes in, one player (right) has pushed an opponent in the back.

2 The opponent falls to the ground. The referee will signal a foul and give a free kick to the fouled player's team. It can be taken by any member of his side.

PULLING
Pulling players' shirts to stop them getting away is a foul.

OBSTRUCTION
Obstruction happens when a player (as here, wearing the bib) unfairly prevents an opponent from getting near the ball.

FREE KICKS

The referee can award one of two types of free kick. A direct free kick can be scored from without anyone else touching the ball. An indirect free kick needs one player of the team to touch it before another can score.

When a team has a free kick, the opponents must move away at least 9.1 metres from the ball. Any player who does not retreat is likely to be shown a yellow card.

This player decides to take a quick free kick. He looks for a team-mate to pass to.

He uses a sidefoot pass to take the free kick.

PRO PLAY

Argentina's Lionel Messi takes a free kick against Venezuela. A top player like Messi can swerve the ball over or around a wall of defenders to score from a free kick.

MAKING THE TEAM

It takes hard work to become good enough to play for your team at school or at an after school club. Training and practice, though, can be great fun as well as a useful way of improving your skills.

PREPARING WELL

1 Before training or a football match, players warm up with some simple jogging.

2 ...and may also prepare by performing heel kicks so that their heels just touch their bottom.

3 Stretching helps to prepare your muscles, such as those in your thighs and arms, for the effort ahead.

4 Some training will focus on improving your speed and fitness. This exercise helps to improve footwork. The players step side-to-side in the spaces between the small cones.

5 Other training will help you to develop your own skills or improve how you play with others. These players are practising their passing skills.

6 Playing football is thirsty work, so make sure you take frequent sips of water.

Concentrate and work as hard in training as if you were in an important match.

Practise skills such as ball control, heading and passing whenever you can.

PRO PLAY

Chelsea's Brazilian player Alex (in blue) jumps for the ball against Liverpool's Jamie Carragher (in red) watched by goalkeeper Pepe Reina. This UEFA Champions League quarter-final second leg match in 2009 ended in a 4-4 draw. Encourage your team-mates during a game and don't give up if your team is losing. Remember, goals can be scored very quickly in football and the game could suddenly turn your way again!

GLOSSARY

attackers
Players in a football team who play closest to the other team's goal. They aim to make and score goals. Attackers are also called forwards.

corner
A kick awarded to the attacking team when the defending team touches the ball last before it goes over the goal line. It is taken from inside the corner quadrant.

defenders
The players in a team who tend to play nearest their own team's goal. Their main job is to stop the other team scoring.

distribution
The way the ball is moved around, especially by goalkeepers throwing or kicking the ball to their team-mates.

dribbling
Running with the ball, controlling it with small taps of the feet.

foul
When a player breaks a law of the game, resulting in the other team being awarded a free kick. Fouls include pushing or tripping an opponent.

free kick
A kick awarded to a team when one of its players is fouled by the opposing side.

goal kick
A kick taken from the goal area usually by the goalkeeper to restart the game. Goal kicks are awarded when the ball crosses the goal line and the attacking team was the last to touch it.

kick off
A kick from the middle of the centre circle used to start each half of a game of football and to restart the game after a goal has been scored.

marking
When players of one team stand close to and guard a player from the other team to try to stop the player winning the ball or getting into a good position to score.

midfielders
Players who have to defend and attack. Midfielders usually play in between their team's defenders and attackers.

obstruction
When one player doesn't go for the ball but uses his or her body to block or stop an opposing player reaching the ball.

penalty area
The large area marked out on a pitch surrounding each goal. If the defending team commits a foul in that area, the referee may award the other team a penalty kick.

sent off
When a player is shown the red card by a referee. The player has to leave the pitch and cannot come back on later. His or her team have to carry on playing with one less player.

shielding
A technique used to protect the ball. Players with the ball shift their body position to keep their body between an opponent and the ball.

tackle
To try to take the ball from an opponent by stopping it or kicking it away.

throw-in
An overhead throw made by one player when the ball crosses the sideline and the other team touched it last.

trapping
To stop the football by placing your foot on the top of the ball.

volley
To hit the ball while it is in the air.

yellow card
Shown by the referee, this is a warning to a footballer about how he or she is playing. A player who receives two yellow cards in a match is sent off.

RESOURCES

BOOKS

Sporting Skills: Football – Clive Gifford, Wayland, 2008
For slightly older readers, this book goes into the techniques and tactics of football.

Football In Focus – Clive Gifford, Watts, 2009
This four-book series looks at different aspects of football including the player skills, tactics and management and the business of running top football clubs.

Training To Succeed: Football – Edward Way, Watts, 2009
This book looks at the lives of a group of teenage footballers who are hoping to make it in professional football.

WEBSITES

http://news.bbc.co.uk/sport1/hi/football/default.stm
The BBC's excellent football webpages include videos of football skills and a Get Involved section listing people to contact for junior football.

http://www.joesoccer.com/info/games.html
A fun website from the United States with simple animations of a large range of different drills and games you can play to improve your skills.

http://www.talkfootball.co.uk/guides/football_skills.html
This website has plenty of information on skills and rules as well as diagrams and videos.

There's a lot to learn when you start out playing football. Most important of all is to remember to have fun! Football is great fun to learn as part of a team. If you have not played before, why not round up some friends so that together you can all... Get Sporty!

INDEX

attackers 4, 5, 14, 16, 23,
    25

backpass rule 9
ball 4, 5, 6, 7, 8, 9, 10, 11,
    12, 13, 14, 15, 16, 17,
    18, 19, 20, 21, 22, 23,
    24, 25, 26, 27
boots 7

coach 29
control 4, 8, 10, 11, 12, 22,
    24, 29
corners 8, 25
crossbar 6, 18

defenders 5, 13, 14, 16, 17,
    20, 21, 22, 23, 25, 27
distribution 21
dribbling 25

fouls 22, 24, 26
free kicks 9, 26, 27

goal 4, 5, 6, 18, 20
goalkeeper 5, 6, 7, 9, 20, 21
goal kick 8

handball 9
headers 16, 17, 29

keepy-uppy 11
kick-off 5, 6
kit 7

marking 14, 23
midfielders 5

passing 10, 11, 12, 13, 14,
    15, 20, 27, 28, 29
penalty 26
penalty area 6, 26
pitch 4, 5, 6, 8, 10, 12, 14,
    21

referees 8, 9, 26, 27

saves 5, 20
scoring 4, 5, 17
sending off 9
shielding 24
shinpads 7
shots 4, 10, 11, 18, 19, 20
sidelines 6, 8

tackling 22, 23
throw-in 8
trapping 10

volleying 19

warming up 28

yellow card 9, 27